Also by Elizabeth Elliott

Poems (1968)

Burn All Night (1998)

Winter Ferry (2008)

plus

¡Cordoba! (1987)
(Spectra's historical music-theatre production)

PLACATE THE JAWS

POEMS

ELIZABETH ELLIOTT

WINTER PRESS
TAVERNIER, FL 33070

www.eelliottpoetry.com

First Edition, December 21, 2010

This book is printed on acid-free paper.

Library of Congress Cataloging-in-Publication Data

Elizabeth Elliott, 1932-

Placate The Jaws: Poems / Elizabeth Elliott. – 1st ed. p. cm.

ISBN 978-0-578-06356-0 (alk. paper)

I. Title.

Cover painting *Open Window* by Bayard Hollins

This book was typeset in Adobe Caslon and Adobe Garamond.
Book, cover and CD insert designed by Kat Moran, Windfall Designs, Stuart, Florida

Website designed by Dianne Steele, Dianne Steele Art and Design, Housatonic, Massachusetts

Audio CD mastered by Greg Steele, Derek Studios, Dalton, Massachusetts

Published in the United States of America by

Winter Press,

Tavernier, Florida 33070

for my four children who are in the thick of it

Elizabeth, Winthrop, Amanda, Alexander

and
my eight grandchildren just getting a taste of it

Page, Laine, Henry, Lucy
Flynn, Charlie, George, Sally

❖

PLACATE THE JAWS

I

II
SHADOWED BY THE NEWS

I

Bramble Pulling

for a clearer of brush

He's been at it now three days,
shedding the slicker,
hooking the clippers on a branch
while he leans

to lift the brush and walk,
blind, to add it to the pile.

When he comes in at six he will ache
the way a road must ache
after it's been broken up,
ripped, graveled

and rolled. But he can see
exactly now, just where the two paths

will soon connect. The brush
and brambles have become a game,
to be considered, to be played
with delicate finesse,

instead of the leap into a
wilderness they seemed at first.

•

He'd forgotten so much when he began. How long things take, for instance.
He can see the clear necessity of connecting

these two paths
to make a circle from the house, expose a hemlock, a thrust of rock,
but this does not convince the brambles
to come easily to his hand.

continued

But wilderness gives way to method.
Method even makes him blind to why he clears.

For a while his only pleasure
lay in this, the clearing.

He forgot the hemlock,
the prow of rock, the paths.
Enough to learn to stack up brush
so it would stay intact when carried
to the pile, to learn

to pick it up before it got so big he'd break his back,
to learn to clip off twigs,

the bushy heads of shrubs,
and leave the trunks for kindling,
to learn not to try to pull up shrubs
but cut them down,
that really, only brambles pull.

•

This is the big thing, learning the character of brambles,
the way they bow down before him,
their arched backs
between him and their stems.

So he has to tackle stems before he grasps the stalks.
The stalk to grasp is the smallest one.
It's green and has the closest hold
upon the plant. The others

may break off but the youngest leads him to the roots. Then sometimes,
if there's a rock beneath, the root lies shallow
and runs up out of the humus
the way a basting thread will run up out of a hem.

The best is when it runs on to its end,
finally sliding clean and smooth
out of the last tunnel of earth,
leaving no way to trace

its history on another spring.
Usually though, the root breaks off
and he knows he's said so long
and not goodbye.

•

Of course it's easy to see the brambles,
they spike the air and lean to catch
his woolen sleeve. But it's those
roots he wants.

Sometimes he gets a root
whose weight says he's

become connected to a tree. So leave that root.
Better to leave the brambles than to hurt
the tree. He sits and looks around.
A little pruning here,
and there, and the hemlock
will show off the rock.

Together they will invite the traveling eye
to journey on around and see the vista change.
Yes, this plain old serene beauty
is worth the sore hands,

the stumble when he walks
toward the house.

•

continued

Two more days and the stunted trees
that grow from old stumps will all be gone.

Two more days and the brambles
will be done,
the green stalks, the older red, the eldest gray,
upended all and growing dry.
Two more days and there'll be a walk to take.

He looks backward to the bramble pile.
Nearly ready to be burned.
Grown dark with roots.

Rage Of The Rich

He'd gone back through the gate to see how the plants were doing,
he'd been the landscape gardener after all;
it still was early, they'd not be here, "I know the rich,
they like to be left alone," he said, "And I like to visit with my work.

"Everything looked fine.
Not quite yet as if the plantings
had been there a hundred years — trees, shrubs, garden.
Not quite. But give it time. I knew they'd both be pleased."

Outside the gate were five Caribbean gardenias.
"Now there," he thought aloud as he slowed the car
and stopped before turning to head uptown,
"Now there was a good choice. And they're full grown.

"God, they smelled! I'll never forget it.
But too strong to grow near a house.
'Better here,' I said, 'Wouldn't Julie love one!
Can't get the likes of this eight storeys up!' "

Leaving the motor running he got out
and picked one of many hundred blooms.
Their scent affected his every pore.
And then: "What are you doing? Hey!

Those are my plants!" The snarl gripped the air.
A car swung and stopped.
"Off season or not, the guy was here."
His voice was rueful now, ashamed a person could be like that.

"What a creep. I tell you.
The way he spoke affected me.
Still does.
Wouldn't be telling you if it didn't."

Eighty Mismatched Socks

No, eighty *unmatched* socks,
overflowing a basket that lives
in the perfect bedroom,
in the perfect house,

on the perfect street,
of the perfect American city
in a very imperfect country
on the day of a very important election.

A collector puts a world together — books or socks,
recipes or votes — whatever once was lost.

In the beginning of the world of socks,
each pair lies cheek to cheek, wedded with a paper ring;
the salesgirl taps the counter top of polished glass
and you decide which pairs you wish to buy —

cheek to cheek and heel to heel
color to color, size to size, stripes, plaids,
they all come home — either today,
some weeks ago, some years from now.

What are the expectations of these pairs?
Be reborn to a grand waltz or a rainy hike?

The plastic T that holds socks close
gets snipped away for the two
separate feet that need them.
Every day a drawer is opened and a choice is made.

One by one each sock is stretched and plunged
to the darkness of a shoe.
And all could still be well
if, when the socks are sent to drown,

be giddied in thrashing soap and space-age spin,
grabbed and tossed to dry in wool-removing heat,

if, when at last dry socks emerge
socks found each other, heel to heel, still paired,
rolled in reunion in a perfect bedroom,
in a perfect house, on a perfect street,

of an imperfect country
on the day of an important election.
But they weren't. They didn't. They aren't.
They never find one another again.

Children And Parents

Little girls lean over their mothers in a fettle
        of fine and secret-sharing love;
Little boys step up beside their mothers
        sulky, slow, too careful of themselves.

        Dominant, impotent, aborting the blood of dreams,
        the Mexican-jumping-bean-fatherdust
        leaps between two spots,
        his stridulous mind to his spasming balls,
        from mind to balls and back again,
        leaping over and over
        the deep and diminishing pool of his heart.

        The mother, left unfastened in a cloud,
        confuses her sex, her heart, her head.

Little girls grow up, can only love the fatherdust,
        dreaming to revive the dead heart back to life;
Little boys grow up, make marriage with the mother,
        she who has engorged his capacity for choice.
Mothers and fathers are strangers in a sojourn,
        faced out of different windows.

        "But he did not become angry,
        for he remembered they were but flesh,
        a wind that passeth away,
        and cometh not again."

Charlie's Mom

Charlie went into his body's house
  One fall,
When he came out next spring,
  Charlie
Was so thin, so pale, so flashed about
  The eye,
The neighbors said the easy thing, that he'd
  Been sick,
Charlie's mother was summoned on the phone,
  She came,
Picked up an old snow shovel, left the umbrella
  Upright
In the tulip bed and went in to see when she
  Came out
She said it wasn't Charles at all, she said it
  Wouldn't
Be her own Charles at all and where had he gone to last
  Fall,
She said this wasn't Charles and so the neighbors
  Fell
To wondering too and only Charlie knew
  For sure.

Christmas Shopping

Bags of peanuts waiting for the trash,
boxed and sliced and bound by yellow tape that reads "Forever,"
rap Nutcracker music banging from above, girls in undershirts
parked over camis, fold and toss undershirts any old how
onto well-made aluminum trolleys.

Undershirts sprawl in six coordinated colors,
glow briefly as they are lifted and held against
knobs of breasts, tossed back to broken arms,
coordinated still though breasts pass on, get shrugged
into black leather jackets made of petroleum. "Mom!"

Every jacket-hidden woman watching over at least one girl, "Mom!"
Imperative demand. Sixty eyes leap to concentrate,
thirty mouths about to say, "Yes?,"
but it wasn't her, it looks like her, they all look like her,
unsmiling knowing eyes, brown floating hair, "Mom! Do you like this?"

A collared undershirt is lifted from the color-coded stack,
soft sister cushion of like on like, now walked along the aisle
dropped once, then married to yet another set of breasts —
money is the least of it. Armpits hanging lax
from hangers crowded on the metal cross.

Hemline has gone up again falls anyway below the soft-tipped pen
the x that marks the moment everything is halved;
each garment thinks of not being the chosen one,
not finding its place on warming flesh,
is it Santah? is it really only Santah?

Wannabe Wannabe

fresh blood on the highway,
fresh fur on the bones

hazing was never like this,
stop answering the phone

you're as cute as can possibly be,
you're a runner who takes the jumps

you've been told there are choices in life,
who said you can't run from the chumps?

take back that swimsuit
come dancing with me instead

texting's a false way to go
if you wannabe happy in bed

Imperious Game

Imperious hand
portrait in diamond left
further in debris than anyone had thought,

plugged down,
no recoil spark,
spoke-shattered and collapsed,

with no long way to move,
no simple way to rise,
to collect

and find itself again with hearts,
the two red suits,
back in the garden of decay

and growth, spades,
and the power of black clubs,
the necessary divisions,

sometimes more than tolerable,
but whether tolerable or
merely necessary,

we couldn't make it without
a whole pack and twos being wild
were no substitute.

Take The Whole Enchilada And Go!

You are protected from surge,
    you know it,
    you bought it yesterday,

    your mother says you always were,
    your father doesn't know what you mean,
and *were* you protected from surge as teen?

Never mind, we can't solve *everything* now,
    you know most of it anyway,
    your body will force you to know the rest,

    meanwhile, your numbers of excuses grow,
    if each excuse was a soldier of war
they'd be liable to die for a decade more.

Go ahead, I'm the one making a hundred dollars an hour,
    What's your very best excuse?
    The one even I can't help you with?

    Ah yes, I see why you shrink and cower,
    your house is a home for unloved rabbits,
all day feeding and cleaning, but havoc for habits.

continued

You need to know; now remember this: you cannot save the world alone,
 you are *not* protected from surge,
 from surge of hate, from rabbits or lice,

 from psychologies bared to a cancerous bone,
 from reason closing its eyes in shame,
knowing it failed and is rightly blamed.

So listen closely,
 you've taken the rabbits,
 you can't go back on them,

 but two things even you must do.
 Clean them, feed them, have loving talks,
and bar the door when the house cat stalks.

Second: you have a closet, surely? For pants and shoes?
 Give these to the rabbits for nests,
 and fill the closet with shelf and chair,

 with a lamp that you carefully choose,
 then just *do* three hours of work, your lifelong habit,
just *do* it, in spite of the noise and the needy rabbits.

Youth

Both cant and canticle, the choirmire of young voices
raise themselves to sing about a world they soon will no:
mini-singers of love and reunion,
but before being tossed out on the old spinal chord,
before exorcising the last mummeries of youth,
they meet and sing to Ailey's bad zittar.

They are fill-harmonic, self-composed,
a frigadoon of love, non obbligato,
an undernsong in the third ecunonical hour of life,
fallacious, fellowcious,
unfledgling tremolo in flannel talk,
not yet packing the foggage of old ideas.

They are a youth-dozen women and men,
long-stemmed and thorny,
no shame-empty love in the boroughs of the heart,
founders of family,
firstlings, fingerlings, boundless forever,
kosher in the labeling room for guests.

Ailey had walked the decks of his court-short ship of Midge,
arguing with her who wanted for them own, an island
amid parables of birds but this never walked into happen;
nevertheless she loved Ailey O'Raunt, wed him,
brought the kosher for the room
and was the wheelwright fletcher of their love's arrow.

Friends came and sat from night to night
on shiny shelves, labeling and liabeling
to know one from one,
turning now off, now on, now hear, now they're,
until it dawned on them and they rent them selves away,
leaving the new coupling alone at last.

continued

And in them a knew world,
an unarmored world was born;
these hands once held aloft the whistling flags,
but savior work pre-veiled, came clear,
they swept the damaged dotage clean,
brought in the books, swore truth;
well-buckled they poured a new foundation.

"Ours"

Eight years ago in the midst of plenty

We turned from "mine" and entered "ours,"

> a country of time not space,
> its wars the flash of one look,
> boundaries reglued as bacon browned,
> revised as patterns were trimmed to suit,
> its garden beds grown to perennial towers.

And on and in till it's over and under,

Chameleon splendor in a timely place.

Ambushed

Two men sit on a terrace,
a twinkled city spread below,
flick their ash into the English ivy,
not aware of growing hungry.
The lean one, a reader of books, is speaking

> "Life is a block of ice
> thrown off by the breaking river;
> we stand upon it as the days go by
> and each day it seems the same;
> it remains rutted and dense and tilted,
> but every day it's whittled down,
> the concentration of river mud is thicker
> and we are always surprised when summer comes."

The second man, leaner still, and long committed
to the spending of a fortune in a millionaire's foundation,
replies in kind,

> "Life is a vapor trail behind a jet;
> strong and clear at first,
> a sweep against the blankness of the sky,
> then petering out to nothing."

But here their ruminations end;
they smell their dinner parading from the kitchen,
and see the glow of candles being lit within.

Alone

Coming toward me on the road,
legs twinkling
in the autumn fall of sun and leaves,

a man with music in his ear,
with exercise of running on the road.
I go past the runner in my car.

We'll never meet. He never knew I passed.
The garden stands oblivious through trees,
purple phlox, red sedum for the drought.

It is itself.
I am here to be myself,
to stay the course.

Whatever is the course,
picked long ago, by me?, to exercise.
Why do I feel crowded?

As though it must take place?
Why must it all take place?
What is the "it"

that must take place?
If we don't act there's no play?
No audience, no play?

Whatever. I'll play to the end,
swing from the satellite we both can hear,
his smooth brown legs twinkling in the sun.

It is itself.
I am here to be myself,
to stay the course.

A Woman Crossing Third

A woman crossing west on Third,
sees someone nicely dressed

striding straight toward her.

She sidesteps to the left.
They'll avoid collision.

But this particular "she" is in a mirror.
She has sidestepped to avoid herself.

(fold here
don't tear)

The architect's joke and risk,
a mirror wrapped around

an office on 39th and Third.
Not losing an ounce of speed

she turns to check her checkered pants.

The mirror shows her eye's confession:
these pants show plenty of expression.

Android

It is a self-powered nanotech,
devoid of microscale devices,
has never been employed
to tap the running power of its blood,
and yet the air of daily breath
that often rushes through its veins,
    quite unconstrained by Saudi whim
    or old deposits uncorked from earth,
such terms from those who know it best,
make death a form of energy
in which it might invest,
could it conserve the power from the flow of blood
to choose the moment for some other birth.

Redwing

swampstruck gymnast,
blackbird whose throat
has brawled since dawn,

rhinal medleys
glottal within
your singer's nose,

garnish gossip,
pleasure your mate,
and maul the scale;

musical dark brawn;

hearing such nodes
and narial notes,
marrows stir and wake,

sombrous oak
stands splashed in ink
of rough fresh songs,

chortling liquor,
signet of spring,
oh lyric shale;

musical, each flake.

In Death Be Proud

in all this heat
and without water
their color was retained

now at last they pass
from cellophane to sink, from sink
to vase in glorious reds

and sunset pinks,
to stand among the kitchen chromes
— beneath admiring eyes.

days later each flower, leaf and stem
is casually thrown down
to lie beneath new wine and old cheese pie.

when colors fade and petals sag
when voices laugh from far above,
quick hands throw down the wine-soaked rag

•

pure sentiment.
even if the farmer's steady knife
had missed you in his blooming field

your glory would be standing
amid the choppings
of your kind, and day would yield

continued

to witless wind and rimless rain
to palsy of some solitary
acres in a stranger's mind.

no purpose but this container here
no strength but what,
this once, for sure, you know

there is no color but what you carry into woe
no will against the headlong hour
no choice but to refuse gray deathless fear

no prize but standing at attention now.

On Stones And Seeds

Is the seed a stone? To be casually tossed aside?
To lie unmoved, resilient as stone?

Can it be tough clay, fine grit?
What if all seed were tossed aside?

What if seeds were used to build a wall?
Think of how a wall would sprout!

Think of a wall coming thick with leaves,
fine stems of thyme, lobelia, willow and weed,
beans and the dark fern,
wheat and the thorned rose,
A wall for museums!

Or what if a million million seeds
were laid out as a gravel path?
The path could only be mud,
a path where even the smallest drops of a mist
would only create more mud.

And the grinders and builders would curse
and learn to go looking for stone,
shouting for joy over intractabilities,
stub-horned desuetudes,
inabilities to transform, impossible to take root.

In this world of grinders and builders
seed would wash to the bottom,

wash to the darkness of good black soil,
and return as grass and food,

return to enrapture and flower
the world grown hard,

so that stone would be beautiful
and the grinders and builders would sigh.

Ocean

There it is,
dressed as usual in one of its best suits —

today it's the winter suit of foam,
great shoulders
of foam-patterned water, foam-decked
seams, laced
and padded, easing themselves
into and out of each other's way, shrugging
and mounting so high

that only a dragger's stovepipe,
heaving along by itself,
in some rear parking lot behind the main attraction,
testifies to the whole Gulf.

Smartly dressed for no one but himself,
appearing louche in the gray, herring-bone monster twills —
but still, it's the muscle, the mass
and the ripple of volume,
the long sleeves and flanks of it, imperturbable power
reaching from Biloxi to Bermuda,
that finally warn you off.

The Philosopher Fails To Anticipate Lunch

This is really not what I wanted to be doing this morning,
I've been taught there's choice, I know there's choice,
I've always carefully chosen. Chosen and known my needs,
the needs of family, friends, community.
As I've matured,
I've learned not to be violent in getting what I choose;
in violence both lose too much.
I've taken space as pleasant substitute.

Space! Yes! And this crowding is very unpredictable,
very rude; someone gross has misread me badly.
What could be in this for that other (whatever that other is)?
It deprives me now of light.

But I still have choice. I see my cousin, poor thing, so maimed,
whom I still detest; see him! I feel him struggling by my side!
But, in our communal dark I'll choose to let old disagreements slide,
treat him in the way *it* should be treating me.

There now. That's better. My cousin's gone. Alone again.
But this dryness — my worst enemy, the air, attacks.
At least the ocean floor is always wet. Life was hard when I was young.
But now I'm old such change as this seems cruelly wrong.

Oh there! Light at least.
Now, water please. I hear it. Hurry please.
I'm a stoic but I must have water if I'm to maintain my calm.
I hear it. I hear delightful bubbles.
I can tell the tide has changed.
A little warm perhaps.

continued

Please hurry. I can't survive this air.
Oh dear, I wonder. I must ask if anyone
who went before me experienced
what I assume are temporary deprivations?
Not that I complain. Such difficulties as these
were probably not considered worth preserving
in the archives of our noble race.
Perhaps. But still, there's nothing I can think of —

"The lobster salad was divine —"

Frost Took Down The Kale

Frost took down the kale last night,
nasturtiums' orange all went out,
the basil's black but

gone to pesto yesterday, (though not enough);
in Ziploc basil's stacked on bones for stock
basil lost to sun and pots.

Did modest nasturtiums hear our words of praise,
and now regret how good it was to eat?
Does kale regret its great gray standing leaves?

November is meticulous in preparation
for what comes next,
merciless to beauty or to authenticated texts.

Let orange leaves and seed-hung flowers,
adorn our salads and our hair,
today luxurious, tomorrow bare.

Flare And Fall

we flare and fall
expand to speed, to breaks and spills,
contract to push again
and strain momentum
on Olympic trails Olympic hills.

while rose whose petals flare
slow-time
without a breath to call "Watch me!"
whose scent gives presence
to the world of bee

becomes
the stunning beauty
of an antique court
the poet's metaphor, the painter's love,
speechless as are full of speech

explosive with Promethean effort
we earn our gold
we earn our praise
our speaking, our Olympic goal
and —
rose both flares and falls as we

Fishes And Loaves

Parsleyed springtime,
radished and vined
with twig and silt,

hilled with seed and
harmonied still
by gift of self,

early blossoms
promise the praise
of salt and grace;

boundaries
well known.

Butter sauces
whipped from the air
and white of egg,

bathe and fold too
shadowy flesh
in bolder light;

safe from distance
home beats as close
as thumb on palm;

comforting
closed space.

Days when distance in you collects,
sees you trowel where your roots are laid,
and bitter fevers in plots you sowed
leer exile from shores becoming pale.

continued

Fish and river,
ocean and fish,
return and tide,

deltas shoal and
enter the flow,
the ebb and flood,

water, river,
fish and the sea,
return upstream;

mouth wet
and mud stopped.

Helm and shell to the rim of heaven,
she is dear to the stem and bar,
sky and sea, all earth and sound
leave her lilied with stars, and clear.

clear to carry
weights of her grief
when sun rhymes dumb,

clear to carry
weights of her love
to the end of days.

singular new strain
new love, her ways
return upstream;

all earth and sound,
one dream.

II

SHADOWED BY THE NEWS

Placate The Jaws

Placate the lower jaws,
inhere the littlest of sparrows,
inclothe his least inheritance
    until the stopper
    of his perfect mouth
lifts and limbo falls
aloft to clinics of prevention.

Oh everywhere! Placate the teeth,
bring them alignment,
loosen their grip on all that's poor,
    on all that's vital,
    that struggle to know
good work; allay and heal
the thirst of the youngest son.

Good work chases the banter of veins,
chases the boy lifting his kite.
The boy runs in the veins
    of his mother
    as all little banters
run in the perfect veins of the mothers,
in all perfect fathers who live love.

Placate the anger of dragons,
the fevered crossroads of death,
make way for the small seeds
    that fall lightly
    to prepared soil,
let them sprout as they know how,
and quietly restore a world reborn.

To The Children Of Those Who Hate Us

deeper than headline news
        our voices to you in friendship
deeper than headline news and the bark of weapons
        our voices come to you across the swift river

        deeper than headline news
        and arms that cradle weapons but not their young,
        women who pack fire and not milk,
        we call to you there is a better way.

deeper than headline news
        we call to you believing you are there
deeper than headline news
        we call to you because the spark between us cannot die.

        deeper than headline news
        and boys gone mad with the power of their guns
        the villainy of rape, abuse and bodies torn,
        our leaders festered in stolen wealth.

deeper than headline news
        the fearless look of friendship in our eyes,
someday we will all choose and love will be our all,
        for love is anchored deeper than the headline news.

FIVE SHORTS

Thank You, Nicholas Kristof

Stable in humidity and heat,
triple-fortified salt:
iodine, iron and vitamin A,
no crop modified by foreign genes,
here's nourishment without a fault.

Kiss Trouble Goodbye

Enable us rabble to raise rice
                    from our own paddies,
                    from our own terraces,
from our own gardens and dreams and hands,

enable that:
kiss trouble goodbye.

Protect Your Frontier

keep happiness on high alert, protect
a balance between top-down intelligent design
and bottom-up autocatalytic market;
keep prices in their rapid flux of free exchange,
and armies will not cross frontiers.

Crowned

warheads on the MX missile,
grouped to form from space a crown

the spikes designed for neither gold nor diamonds,
designed for military obsessed with getting more

this crown became the goal to which men swore
and people of the earth were heard no more

Love Blue Jays

If all that's left
            is blue jays,
if the rail feeds none
            but blue jays
well, count that blessing
            love blue jays.

Arouse The Sheep

Arouse the sheep!
Wipe off your best sermons!
Great plenitudes of stars
graze the edges of Eden.

Arouse the sheep!
The strongholds of desire shift,
new ways need room
for new lowering of the bars.

How can we awaken to so much?
How take in the discourse,
the requirement for depth
in each and every word?

How shake the meaning of "stand"
until its jewels and its sins
push loose the mouth closed,
hard, on the spine of force?

The time for delay is over and gone,
the time for new love is now,
though we tinker on the edge of doom,
we will wake in Eden — from sleep.

Every Man From His Own Trench

What do they say in the trenches,
When guys are alone and no wench is
        or wasn't until war became equal
        and no one survives for the sequel
now that blood and not wine is what quenches.

What quenches the soul, what shrivels and quibbles,
the quest of the questing friend,
        can't be mandated away by robes on high benches,
        by shrinks or by will, by Hillary or Bill,
a Florida room or a house on the blustering blueberry hill.

What quenches our thirst in the trenches
may not present us the First,
        but even if Last it's not Worst,
        and we can't feel accursed
if we're still alive in our crazy expensive-dug trenches.

In An Early Shroud

more than gentle
more than proud
is pity for those young
close-covered in an early shroud

and if the drum's not ready
to call us through its gate
we hear it soft and steady
for our children, friends and mate

stern and holy are the roads
where innocence is felled,
the gentle, furious and proud,
the gorgeous life — for tokens quelled

be still oh pity in the heart,
turn now your mind to reason
and answer what it means
when killer's act spells treason

If They Are Mad

If they are mad, be you not mad,
when sense pours bloodied from their greedy lips
be Hamlet-mad and play for existential time,
find markings on the stones where there are none,
refuse the knowledge and beneficence of rain
even as you fill your pockets with its wash and blast,
point to where the lightning sears
the hand that claims to feed the babe.

Conjoin such madness to a plan
that lets you vanish from their overheated toil;
cavelike, descend to restful anonymity
and give consent to every simple, mindless thing.

All things revert from shame,
the lame will rise and never be the same.

Just Get Brady Mad

Time is the bent bow
and the arrow returns to the archer.

Here is the great divide,
here in the wind of this screaming hill.

The blackbirds have returned;
a flock went chirring overhead today.
It's early March.

A second flock lands on the unleaved elm.
In excess exhilaration it takes off again.
Whose side will we be on?

The earth breathes.
Here in the north another spring prepares.

In two more weeks
the birdsong will be heard from every side.

•

But my children have not had children.
The tide toward life has not come in.
Will we be too late?
How many will be "good Germans,"
docile, obedient to the boss,
riveting planes, sealing bombs,
answering phones, serving food,
ordering pads and pens,
mopping the floor where the button is.

Who is brave enough
to lock the room where the button is,
to throw the key away?

"No admittance." That's all it takes.
Signs on all the button-rooms saying,
"No admittance."

When we finally know what we want,
it's always easy to achieve.
It's just a matter of work and time.

But this death, these bombs,
they have us all enthralled,
entombed in power.

We are hypnotized, not free to be direct.

•

And yet it's only old Sam Brady
standing there on guard.
He ain't so special.
He pisses and farts like all the rest.
It's only old Sam.
It would only take one Sam Brady,
to throw the key away, and suddenly

we would all begin to go clean again.

Violations

death by numbers,
casual dress for death's disguise,
numbers and more numbers
added and padded to the carnival sum.

our troops today, this week;
our collateral, their daughters
sons, a marketplace; their mothers
people looking from a roof.

our troops lined up in rows and silent in the grass.

the shock of red and black
is not a woman sweeping crumbs,
we bear this truth obscured,
blind to its unsurprising toll.

Outside Postnet

Why does the young man limp?
He is tall, he wears the required gear —
the pockets around to the back,
and down to the knee.

He walks fast,
as fast as he is able,
his face humiliated with effort.

But he has a place to go,
or he had a place to go,
he has a place to go.

•

Is heartbreak for this young man
what gives such pain? Let go my mind,
free it to the edges of the world and back
and see there all the shapes and shadows,
all the limps and twisted arms,
the shot, bright, crazy, still connecting eyes
of those who have a place to go,
had a place to go, a thing to do,

have still a place to go, a thing to do.
Weep for these.
Weep for these and know it's done.

Scorpion, Don't Starve Here

Sweeping blown leaves, dark scorpion
was caught making for the terrace sill,
he turned to skitter back across the kitchen floor,
heading for the shelter of an inner hall.

No, not here!
Better to be snapped in a saber beak,
to vanish into change
than to starve here,

in this place so clean, well lighted.

Many Mansions

Have I not enough of these? When will you study me?
Why quit because you hear of home?
Perhaps you'd rather hear of quivers to my bow?
Fires from the sky?
Shocks and struggles in the muscle?
And have I not enough of blood
to bleed for why I love you still
even in the damping of your conscience,
in your preference for the neighbor's ear,
in all the little safeties of your life?

Have I not enough of various pains?
Of appetites to reward the hungers that you crave?
Why ask me to produce more proof when miracles fall,
one by one, appropriate comets from the psychic sky?
Oh staring savage, startled Essex on the run,
disgrace to Nature that has no choice,
but gives you models of what you might become,
why do you so belittle
all you actually are?

Have I not enough of shells and pearls and ice receding?
And still did I not grant you choice
as to no other was choice so granted?
Do I now regret? Oh how I regret.
How I could so easily
snatch it back,
begin again but worlds away.
Before the earth
you claim to love —

III

Before You Close The Lid

Before you close the lid
say thank you for me to my feet,
    always cheerful for a tramp,
    confused by dancing orders from above.

Say thanks to knees that yanked me in the way that I must go,
their complexity but sign of high ambition,
    knees now gone to pasture they deserve,
    I linger but their work's complete.

My hips, replaced so long ago,
I always thanked for arts of love,
    but reckless passions are so few
    cracked hips with others lie clean in bony piles.

Pelvis and all that waits to throb,
I beg you, open the windows of my mind,
    visit me once more to wilder scenes,
    those feral loves, the children who came slipping through.

Before you close the lid,
remark as on you pass,
    how time alone now seals the passage
    to all I thought and all I did.

•

You must, for I no longer can,
thank the pleasure of my nose and mouth,
    the scrupulosity of words,
    the way my wrist and mouth knew poems,

continued

the joining and rejoining of sense and sound,
of all that's past and might still come,
        the details and the thought today,
        unique and apt to all my solitary hours.

Oh yes, before the lid is closed,
say thank you for the time I had,
        though time itself took all I did,
        though time itself takes all I have.

Behind what hair, within what skull,
upon what rumpled pillowcase,
        is not where I'll be found.
        Don't look for me I'll not be found.

•

All giving and all taking once so intense
with glorious or with fatal speed,
        connectors working between hand and neck,
        now lie inert below my face.

Only belly brought pleasure to the last,
scornful of dangerous swell to vein,
        mind surrendered to one last pretense,
        to curried lamb, risotto and to crème brulée.

My hands have gone before me,
as in a sense they've been my eyes,
        holding, releasing, protecting shape,
        translating heart for each surprise.

Before you close the lid,
remark as on you pass,
        how time alone has put a stamp
        on all I thought and all I did.

•

Thank you to all these forever,
(though pumping heart and fading mind,
    today reject the peace "they" counsel me to know,
    instead construe and urge the very words

to yet betray my leaving —
I'd milk away to racing silks and jockeys still unknown,
    yes! to beat against the wind,
    race north beneath all lifting bars.)

But no, I myself laid that to rest,
so let it be, another day may come,
    (whoever says it won't
    has really not one clue of what there Is.)

To my self, whatever 's left of such a wondrous thing as "self,"
I thank, honor, and ever bid its soul
    to pure acceptance,
    and to you God's blessing, as you close the lid.

What Matters

it's not whether the sumac
                rocks with the jay or crow,
or if anyone has noticed it before.

it's not whether some squirrels
                take all the other's share,
or if anyone has chased them off before.

it's not whether you are in a place
                like all the others,
and everyone is doing exactly as they always have.

it's what you make of this. That matters.

Loss Of Light

There is a moment when the trees are black from loss of light,
and water by whose edge they stand
is filled with the brilliance of the fallen sun,

and in this moment one understands the unconscious,
how it stands by us even when we need it least,
when the sun is strong and day fair,

when we are not imagining questions or questioning answers,
and we think the water is for our boat to cross over on,
it is, only it is not that boat.

High Summer, Tyringham

The first clear day, high summer,
windows wide, screens in place, from down the hill

— across the field,
to where the meadows,
like a wrap hold hills
and woods, unwittingly
provide the view —

we hear their voices as they mow;
they meet a moment and go still. And then:

Mackie's voice appreciating
some remark of Heamon's spoken
from under his wide-brimmed hat.
Laughter. We don't hear words,
only the sound of voices.

Voices clear as water
or the liquid flute of evening thrush.

Though on this Sunday morning the voices fade.
The two machines begin to work a further slope;
the genial figures call and answer,
pause and call, but from far away.

Deep summer. The familiar voices of content.
Deep winter merely myth.

Appropriate Ambition For A Parrot

When I fly,
with whom and where,

how often leave my perch
to cleave the always breezy air,

is not an appropriate source
of reprimand and blame;

my one concern this Christmas lunch
is: do I still retain the knack

to ricochet beyond
the nervous voices of alarm,

the shelves of heirloom bric-a-brac,
and, having wreaked no harm,

still reach the top of that strong,
but oh so distant picture frame,

that so desirable
stout oasis on an empty wall?

•

Don't scold the cage-bound parrot
for his longings still to fly,

as soon withdraw the carrot
if a stick is found nearby.

FOUR SONGS

1

Just A Detour

Just a detour off the main road,
just a little walk in what they call a park,
a meadow with a little stream,
a bank with flowers in the grass,
and in front of where I sit, that mountain pass.

That was all you were,
all I'd gone a'askin' for,
just a detour off that long main road,
a day of laughter, a night in bed,
I wasn't looking for a change I said.

But now I see that plain white church
in silhouette against the hills,
and I know that detour was my home,
but I left those flowers in the grass,
got lost along that mountain pass.

2

Dancing In The Valley Of The Dolls

There's dancing in the valley of the dolls,
And the ladies swing their legs again,
The gents are up and know their way around,
There's dancing in the valley and there's rain.

I hollered but you didn't hear,
And all the tongues were clacking in the night,
I hollered but you didn't hear,
As you were getting out of sight.

Yes, I hollered till the wind felt bad,
And hightailed my words to you,
My words were heard in Charles Towne,
But my words weren't heard by you.

Oh pardon me my dark transgression,
I waited for you on that windblown pier,
I waited till an empty boat came back,
I waited till you'd disappeared.

So when there's dancing in the valley of the dolls tonight,
When all the ladies dance and play,
Remember if you will out there,
You ain't a'lay'n where you once lay.

Honey, tonight when the ladies feel no pain,
And the gents are up and gettin' around,
I won't be lie'n where you once lay,
And I won't be lie'n in no cold ground!

3

Indium Blues

I got them cyanide blues,
my entrails knows 'em from the past,
those days I learned that you were lost,
those cyanide,
those extra Prussian blues.

Don't want no cancer blue to come,
no cobalt dancing in that witch's ring,
maybe those two old oxides,
black manganese and sister indium
will give me a blues it's safe to sing.

Out of all that heat and hurt,
with indium and stars you'll come,
my entrails wait to hear your step,
your voice that says, "I'm home again."
Betcha my blues won't ask, "Where from?"

No need to know particulars,
no need to knock those bruises down again,
I'll take you just a sittin' here,
I'll take you in starlight or in rain,
two blues in harmony without no blame.

I've got them harmony-blue-moon blues,
those particular hummable sky-blue-blues,
indium rhythm along one track,
you takin' your turn and you turnin' back,
together we sing good hungrier indium blues.

4

All In White Linen

All in white linen white linen rode she,
couvre-chef, wimple headrail and crown,
hands able to knead out a pie for his table,
as all in white linen she rode into his town.

Boiled leather cuirass over chain-mail and tunic,
ready for war and for war rode he,
rode out in chain-mail came back in a shroud,
all in white linen came all of his armor, all in white linen came he.

Did her braids to her knees sport tips of long metal?
Did her mantle sufficiently hide steel-webbed sleeves?
Her girdle of mail? Her heart of deception,
her milk of inception as all in white linen she leaves?

Illness Rests

Illness rests within the frame,
Patient of its fate to wreak its ill,
Knowing it is just exactly as it is,
For each particular heart and will.
Determined by some chosen quirk of fate,
It knows its power to strike and kill.

Patience is all it needs to spend and save,
To make a patient and to dig a grave.

Is Death The Proud Upstart?

Is death the proud upstart it appears,
a presence of such casual power,
its dismissal shows contempt for tears?

Or is death the tactful comforter, the shears
whose kindly blade releases ties
we usually praise, both truth and lies.

Perhaps one's death is merely pause
between our lying down and why we rise
between perfection and perfection's flaws.

Lunch Guest

I saw death roll its eyes and pounce,
as if its promise was but ruse
to lure the rube
into its sleep of life.

Peculiar gait it had,
as if a limp itself was play,
and smell, as of some laundry
that could not dry.

Like pickled herring
we knew our time was up
but — this was strange —
death said he could not stop.

Don't Cremate Me

When I die don't cremate me
        I want to lie
        on my stomach
        in a coffin
        and have you sit
        beside me your
hand rubbing my naked back.
When neighbors come to see
        how beautifully
        I'm embalmed
        they will see me
        at the happiest
        moment of my life
(So useful not to believe in death.)

Does It Have To Be Like Everything Else?

The last movement
doesn't *have* to sound as if it's a separation and the end.

Does it? Trumpets in dotted eighths
don't *have* to signal the final tympatic stir, accelerating drumble

that comes before the silence. Do they?
Must we be shocked with unearned surprise until we notice the relief?

•

But yes, even though the end is near
it seems the brass *must* climb the challenge of yet another theme.

However, note: uncurious violins
follow the ruminations of a flute to Indian summer joy.

If sadness follows,
well, sadness follows all days of mammographic obedience to the rules.

•

The beaded sweat flies,
drumroll accepts a very close shave, violins soar and let go.

Chaste, The Priest

Chaste the Priest played piano parsely,
complained the singing stirred too thick a brew,
but when they cried and said there was another,
he laughed a finger-tipped content and said he wasn't through.

He played, this Chaste, as though the devil knew his name,
he noticed not his floiyns were turning blue;
oh try, they cried, to break into the crust of love,
our hearts abrokenly detain desire,
oh give us feeling and the healing of your pain.
But Chaste, wind-driven Priest, still said he wasn't through.

Slowly, and before their very eyes,
he quickened down into an ancient screw,
tongue-tapped curslings came pitched toward their ears,
overloading hearses, waddling of a runic few;
too terrified to voice complaint they sat to see the living through
and heard the windthrip rattle in his guttered throat.

They leaned to sift the shaftings of his sloak and moan,
and moon, just then appearing on the sill,
sleeved forth his rueing bloat and torment sailed a dream-pitched sea;
he lived each terror of all former time, piano-played all keys,
piano-plumbed the living depths of lies,
piano-played his fearfuls into brew.

continued

While moon belingered long
they stayed to hear exhaustion tapping out a silent plea,
a stillness startled dimly in the din of death,
for they who sat heard tides that breathed
stagnation fresh as prisoners set loose among the wolves,
and woke to hear a swallow dipping in the wings of song.

They traveled with him that long-lasting ever-eve,
until his hands fell limply to his side;
ghosts begathered and then left,
left forward, and left up, left played
as right followed failing to insist on will,
as right followed left and found that neither was afraid.

What night was this when Chaste the Priest played on and on?
What brood-mare reveries from off his soul were pruned?
Can it be that in the laundry of a song
there is the linen for the wound?

Human Magic

for Susan Rodgers's sculpture

She presents us with air to watch,
to notice wreaths around our head.

She notices the colors we breathe,
speak through, and when yellows go drifting away

she frames the blue just where we forgot to look.
But looking, we remember she put it there.

She won't overwhelm or withhold,
or exile the air to a permanent pink,

she never carves it from things which already exist.
Yet air's only half of all she streams.

She sets air in a color afloat in a cup,
in a tree, in the flight of a bee,

she wraps up the fingers of a tired sun,
plays cat-cradle till evening's well begun.

Air settles wherever she shakes it out,
wherever she strings it up or hangs it about.

She can stretch it from roof to the lowest sill
with the style of a hummingbird always on show.

Her wires bend to the flair of appearing,
to a thrum and a tremble of yellow string,

and no gate, nor a ring, or anything more
can speak to the footfall and high-rise she brings into being.

Habit Of Music

You wear the habit now, of music,
know it, not in your ears alone,
nor even in your heart,
but in your neck and in the tension of your hands,
the way your back feels as you walk the falling slope,

and know,
that with, but one outward change of skin,
you could,
without disruption,
become music.

Flattened, pinned against the sky,
your ear cupped toward the sun,
you hear the flatulence of chord,
the stirring tongues of tune.
And know

that if you could adjust the key
a fraction,
but a quantum hair,
there'd be nothing to hear but music,
nothing to see save only,

music,
nothing to know but
music. Even now,
before this comes, all is —
music.

Copies of *Placate The Jaws* can be ordered at:

- **Artisan Books & Bindery:**
  509 Pendleton Point Road
  Isleboro, ME 04848
  (207) 734-6852
  www.artisanbooksandbindery.com

- **The Bookstore:**
  11 Housatonic Street
  Lenox, MA 01240
  (413) 637-3390
  bookstoreinlenox.com

- **Amazon.com**

Hear and read 10 poems from each of Elliott's four books at:
www.eelliottpoetry.com

Elizabeth Elliott

Placate The Jaws is Elliott's fourth book of published poetry. From 1976 to 1981 she taught the craft of poetry in the Gallatin School of New York University where she devised a system of fourteen ideograms for the understanding and comparing of English-language rhythms, whether of prose or poetry in any time period.

With composer Seth Cooper, Elliott co-founded, and for a decade directed, Spectra, a non-profit, inter-disciplinary and cross-cultural performing arts organization. Some of Spectra's venues were Hudson, New York, Merkin Hall in New York City, and The Asia Society. In 1987 Elliott's *¡Cordoba!,* was produced by Spectra in Hudson, New York. Utilizing several nationalities of musicians, singers, dancers and actors from New York City, the music-theater piece, *¡Cordoba!* was an historical condensation of the world's first high civilization. Enduring for many centuries, this was the first time, but hopefully not the last, in which Jews, Moslems and Christians lived and worked together as creative equals. For much of this period Europe was in the throes of "the dark ages" and it was thus to Cordoba, Spain that philosophers and poets, teachers and musicians, creative people of all kinds, were drawn.

Acknowledgements

WB Yeats writes of the conflict between life and the work. I am grateful to the following people who stayed out of the way of the work but made its reality possible: Mary Zander who published *Burn All Night* and Greg Steele, the tech wizard responsible for mastering the audio CDs found inside back covers of the books. My current website was designed by Dianne Steele, and I owe special thanks to Bill Dimbat, John Berthet and Page Clason who provided ongoing technical support. Kat Moran originally designed *Burn All Night* in 1992 and has continued the association by designing and producing this volume and compact disc as well as the 2008 publication of *Winter Ferry.* Thank you all.

Then there are those who understand the conflict between life and work and insist on both, especially my husband, Clint.

Why include the work of a painter in a book of poetry? Poetry is an art complete in itself. So, obviously, is painting. And the illustration of poetry is its own art, creating a format where poems and artwork are closely juxtaposed. Does an introduction to the cover artist take away from the poems? I do not believe so. In this case, the cover painting was carefully chosen from the work of a young modern painter because of a sensibility that I felt spoke strongly to the poems, elusively and without even a hint of illustration. It wasn't until *Winter Ferry* was published with a cover painting by Evelina Kats, that I realized how much richer that book would have been if a few more of Kats's paintings had been reproduced as Hollins's have been. To my mind two entirely different arts are being placed near each other but with a clear and strong physical separation between them. I feel, and hope they enhance and prolong the experience for the reader and viewer. Comments would be welcome on my website at: **www.eelliottpoetry.com.**

Here then, on this and the next three pages, is a short introduction to Bayard Hollins and his work.

BAYARD HOLLINS, *1966–*

Hollins: "explores the link between abstraction and figurative representation," loves what he calls the "rawness of nature," and leaves figures and objects mostly undefined so that the imagination of his viewers is stimulated. His work is both primitive and sophisticated.

From 1984 to 1996 Hollins was educated at art institutions in Florence, Italy and in Spain with two years at the New York Academy of Art. He has had ten one-man shows, been in twelve group shows, and exhibited in the Aspen Museum of Art twice and the Dallas Museum of Art once. He lives in Colorado with his wife and two children.

Three of Hollins's paintings can be seen on the next pages as well as others on his website: **www.bayardhollins.com.**

Bayard Hollins, ***The Beach****, 2008, Mixed media on canvas, 64" x 64"*

Bayard Hollins, ***Three Graces,*** *2008, Mixed media on panel, 32" x 24"*

Bayard Hollins, ***Pan Fried,*** *2008, Mixed media on canvas, 48" x 60"*

Praise for Elliott's *Burn All Night:*

"The precisions of Dickinson and Moore, their somewhat tactful measurings of the sublime (important not to intimidate it!), and, farther back, the elegiac smile of Herrick and Vaughan's starry night inform Elizabeth Elliott's poetry, for our pleasure and profit. Hers is a strong and original voice that speaks from the center of the English poetic tradition."

– John Ashbery

Burn All Night is a maturely disciplined volume, the work of a refined sensibility and an authentic stylist. There are poems here that sustain repeated rereading, and that should endure."

– Harold Bloom

I was greatly taken by [*Burn All Night*]'s wit, eloquence and lyricism. Some of the poems have the incantatory power of Blake or Yeats, a quality I miss in most contemporary poetry. Others are wonderfully rich in sensory detail.

– Roger Gilbert

I like the boldness, the wildness of these poems. It is so clear the writing comes from the heart, allowing nothing to get in the way of the primitive energy, the impulse. Oh there is plenty of craft too, technique enough, but the poems have a kind of spontaneity and momentum —

– Daniel Mark Epstein

Poems cut to the quick and are so precise and dear as to seem inevitable.

– Victoria Abrash

Simply wonderful: fresh, original, distinctive and distinct. Anybody who knows that to the bud the blossoming sounds like thunder knows all one needs to know in order to burn all night.

– Frank Fagan

Unsolicited letters from early readers of *Winter Ferry:*

I read it all in one sitting, handing it off to Polly saying, "Read this one!" I don't think I've ever read poetry with such eagerness to know "what next?"
– **Susan Rodgers,** sculptor

To find a poet who has not abandoned the romance of language, who doesn't spend her time making sure she is severe is a great blessing for an old Victorian communist like me. And *Winter Ferry* itself is an important poem.
– **Val Coleman,** writer and civil rights worker

The poetry always grabs me by the throat!
– **Richard Lipez,**
foreign affairs journalist and,
as Richard Stevenson,
author of gay mystery books

The only poem that in its overthrow of the paradigm, threw me over as well, was "In Praise," but I take that as an indication of my limitations. An Elizabethan (no pun intended) would find it joyful, as it clearly is.
– **Alice Wohl,**
independent scholar
and translator of *Bellori's Lives*

The poems are strong. During the reading I felt pulled mentally and emotionally to extreme and different places. Recovery time would have been in order.
– **Monica Zanen,** painter

Whether talking about love, sex, growing old, family, nature or obliquely about current politics, Elizabeth Elliott's elevated, almost archaic language, her elegiac tone and her piercing, relentless eye bring into stark relief the angst and quandaries of the post-modern age. She is always in control of cadence and syntax. Her love of sound as well as sense sings through the urgency of these poems.
– **David Budbill,** poet